THE PAIN WE HOLD INSIDE

Grieving Parent

DIONNE MACK

Copyright © 2021 Dionne Mack.

All rights reserved. No part of this book may be used or reproduced by any means, graphic, electronic, or mechanical, including photocopying, recording, taping or by any information storage retrieval system without the written permission of the author except in the case of brief quotations embodied in critical articles and reviews.

This book is a work of non-fiction. Unless otherwise noted, the author and the publisher make no explicit guarantees as to the accuracy of the information contained in this book and in some cases, names of people and places have been altered to protect their privacy.

Archway Publishing books may be ordered through booksellers or by contacting:

Archway Publishing
1663 Liberty Drive
Bloomington, IN 47403
www.archwaypublishing.com
844-669-3957

Because of the dynamic nature of the Internet, any web addresses or links contained in this book may have changed since publication and may no longer be valid. The views expressed in this work are solely those of the author and do not necessarily reflect the views of the publisher, and the publisher hereby disclaims any responsibility for them.

Any people depicted in stock imagery provided by Getty Images are models, and such images are being used for illustrative purposes only. Certain stock imagery © Getty Images.

ISBN: 978-1-6657-0716-9 (sc)
ISBN: 978-1-6657-0717-6 (e)

Library of Congress Control Number: 2021909947

Print information available on the last page.

Archway Publishing rev. date: 6/1/2021

Introduction

As sure as there is life, there is death! I had heard that statement many times throughout my life, but I never expected it to hit so close to home. That was true until I was faced with the worst possible and unexpected nightmare of my own. Unfortunately, this is a nightmare that I will never wake up from. How can I? No mother expects to lose a child and, honestly, how can you ever prepare for such a tragedy? Moreover, how can you move forward when you have more questions than answers?

One

Have you ever just felt like something was wrong? Like something terrible was going to happen but you couldn't put your finger on what it could be? I like to call it a sixth sense, where your mind receives an unknown message that you cannot explain but you can feel all around you. That thing that you cannot see or feel—it's just there, like the brush of wind across your face on a breezy day. That is exactly the feeling I had when I woke up on the morning of November 17, 2010. It wasn't the typical hump-day, Wednesday-morning blues for me; I woke up with an overwhelming feeling of sadness and an extreme desire to pull the covers over my head, like a child who knows there is a monster under the bed or in the closet. I didn't know why I was overwhelmed with fear and sadness, but I couldn't shake it.

My friend called me to say good morning, as he did every morning; I almost didn't answer the phone, but I did not want to be rude. He kept asking me if I was OK, because he could hear something in my voice. I told him that I felt like something was going to happen and that I couldn't shake the urge to cry, but I didn't know why. His intuition led to probing questions that I found hard to answer. How can you explain something to someone when you don't understand it yourself? He and I continued our conversation of encouragement, like we did every day before going off to work. But for me, the depressed state of mind was so bad that I skipped work and let my son drive himself and his sisters to school because I couldn't make myself get out of the bed. I didn't feel like talking to or seeing anyone. I just wanted to lie in bed and cry, although the tears would not fall.

I spent most of the day lying in bed in the dark room with my phone on silent, trying to mute the world and that awful feeling. The television was on, but there was barely any sound coming from it. I caught myself looking at the TV a few times, realizing my mind had drifted, and I didn't even know what I was watching or if I was watching anything at all. My eyes were open, but my mind was in a dark, distant place. Later that day I got up and showered, hoping that would make me feel better and also make me look somewhat presentable before the kids came home from school. I made my way to the kitchen and threw together a quick meal for dinner that I had just finished by the time the kids walked in. They ate dinner, and everything around me seemed to be OK in spite of that awful feeling I still had that continued to float in the atmosphere around me. The kids did their homework and joked around with each other while I lay in bed watching TV.

Around five thirty that evening my son asked if he and my nephew could go play basketball at the local recreation center, just as he had the day before. Ironically, when he asked to go play basketball the day before, I told him no because he had been coughing all day, and I didn't want him having an asthma attack. To this day I ask myself why I let him go that day. Maybe it was his sweet disposition and irresistible charm that made it hard for me to say no to him two days in a row. Whatever the reason was, I agreed to let him go if they were back in time for Bible study, which would have allowed them about an hour to play basketball. Actually, I had no plans on going to Bible study, but I had told my sister that she could drive my car to church, so it was imperative that they be back in time to shower and get dressed. To pass time and try to get my mind off that weird feeling, my sister, my daughter, my niece, and I all piled in the bed and started watching a Denzel Washington movie, *John Q.*

I had seen the movie several times before, but it's just one that seems to get better the more you watch it. *John Q* was one of the best examples of the lengths a parent would go to in order to protect, fight for, and save their child. I didn't know that I was about to be in a real-life movie, tested to the extreme limits of parenting. We were about thirty minutes into the movie when my fourteen-year-old daughter came into the room frantic. With the look of fear on her face and despair in her voice she said, "Mommy, Tyrell's not breathing!"

She continued to say that phrase over and over as she held the phone to her ear and jumped up and down. I thought she was playing a really bad joke on me, so I asked her who was on the phone.

"Justin!" she replied.

The look in her eyes and the fear in her voice told me that it wasn't a joke. It was like someone had punched me in the chest, knocking the wind out of my body to a point that it felt like my heartbeat had slowed down. I told her to tell my nephew to get off the phone and call 911. My sister started wrangling the kids and telling everyone to hurry and put on their shoes. We were moving so fast, and it was like everything around me disappeared. I was moving, but all I could see was silhouettes of things. Nothing was clear, and all of the sounds around me were like muffled echoes.

I jumped up and threw on some shoes while my sister yelled to all the kids to get in the car. I was shaking like a leaf while trying to remain levelheaded. I don't remember getting in the car, nor do I remember the drive to the recreation center, which was less than five minutes away. Everything happened so fast that I didn't even realize that I left my fourteen-year-old daughter at the house scared and alone. To this day, I don't know why she didn't get in the car. My mind was in a distant place, and my heart felt like it was in my stomach. All I knew was I had to get to my son. As I pulled up to the recreation center, everything seemed to move in slow motion. It was like I had an out-of-body experience, one that would become common; I just didn't know it at the time. It felt like I was standing outside of my own body watching things unfold, but I couldn't react to it. As my sister and I walked into the recreation center, leaving the kids in the still-running car in front of the building, I remember asking everyone I saw to show me where the gym was. There were people standing and walking around, but no one was responding to me. *Do they know that there is an emergency taking place inside their facility?* I was wondering. *Maybe this is a bad joke that my son and nephew decided to play.* From the looks of things and the lack of response I was getting I just knew I was going to whip their butts if they were pulling a prank.

Finally, a little boy walked up and told me to follow him. We walked a few feet before turning a corner, and in less than a minute we were approaching the gym. Again, I don't know what I was expecting, but I just knew it couldn't be as bad as my nephew made it sound on that phone call. As I walked into the gym, I saw my son lying on the cold gym floor. No shirt on, no one helping or caring for him. He was just lying there. I felt like all of the breath was being sucked out of my body, and I leaned against the wall to regain my disposition. I scanned the room, and there were people standing around and sitting on the bleachers.

"He's not breathing," I told my sister, as if I needed confirmation.

She grabbed my hand and said, "Come on, sister; it's OK."

I looked her in her eyes. "He's not breathing." I began to gasp for air. "His stomach isn't rising and falling!" My hands were shaking like a leaf on a windy day; my heart was pounding so hard it felt like it was going to come out my chest. I was in shock and didn't want to believe that this was actually happening to me. There was no way my baby was lying there helpless and not breathing. My mind moved at the speed of light, and in a matter of seconds every moment of my son's life flashed before my eyes. I immediately remembered the first flutter in my stomach when I carried him in my womb. I remembered the smell of his breath when he was a baby, the smiles he gave me on his first day of kindergarten when I dropped him off for his first day at the "big boy school," as he called it. I remember his first touchdown on the football field, the first record he set in track and field, and his laughter and protective nature when it came to me. Most importantly, I remembered the way he looked me in my eyes and told me he loved me just before he walked out of the house.

As my sister pulled on my arm, we ran toward my son. All the while I was shaking my head no. *No way this is happening; why aren't they doing anything to help him?* Those were the thoughts that ran through my head as I approached my son.

People were everywhere, but I couldn't understand why no one was trying to help him. My son, my only son, who was lying there in need of help, but not one person was doing anything. As I kneeled beside him, the first thing I did was checked for a pulse. It was there—faint, but there. So many thoughts were going through my mind. I kept thinking back to the CPR classes I had taken years ago as I tried to convince myself to remain calm instead of panicking so that I could remember what I needed to do next. Would I know how to properly do chest compressions? This wasn't like the CPR dummies I had practiced on all those years ago. But I had to try, so I started doing chest compressions, tears falling from my eyes like a rapid waterfall. I stopped the compressions, leaned down, and lifted my son's head toward my face. Cheek to cheek, I whispered in his ear, "Breathe, baby. Breathe for Mommy." It was at that moment that one of the employees from the recreation center, who had been standing over my son's body from the time I walked in, tapped me on the shoulder and said, "Keep his airway open!" Although he was correct, I looked at him with the hopes that my stare would burn a hole in him, considering the fact that he hadn't been trying to help my son when I'd walked in. There had been two men standing over my son when I'd walked in, and I'd heard one them say "Jesus" as I kneeled beside my son. I guess he thought calling on the name of the Lord would be more beneficial than trying to help my son or calling 911.

As angry as I was at his ignorance, I knew I needed to focus my attention on my son. With my hands still shaking hard and fast, I kept doing chest compressions, although I felt like I didn't have enough strength to properly do them, and I didn't feel like what I was doing was working. My baby still was not responding! I kept rubbing my hand across his face and touching his stomach, hoping to feel for the rise and fall that happens as a person breathes in and out. Nothing! *Dear God, help me, give me strength*, is what I kept thinking as I did compressions. "Where the hell are the paramedics?" I said. I had never been so scared in my life. I felt helpless, and I needed to be the hero in that moment, the superwoman my son always thought I was.

I could hear the sirens, but I couldn't understand why they weren't there yet. It didn't make any sense to me. How was I able to get to the recreation center before the ambulance? They should have been there before me, right? I jumped up and ran toward the double doors, hoping that my standing in the doorway would make the ambulance magically appear. Just as I reached the door, the paramedics were coming up the hall pulling a stretcher. I kept saying, "My son isn't breathing. Please hurry." I followed them to my son's lifeless body and stood in disbelief as they tried desperately to resuscitate him.

I wanted to scream to the top of my lungs as I watched helplessly. But I stood silently, shaking and praying. *God, please don't take my baby! God, please don't take my baby!* I kept asking the paramedics why he wasn't responding, but they wouldn't answer me; their jobs were to focus on my son, not me. One paramedic was doing chest compressions; another one was putting the air bag over my son's mouth and squeezing it. They were in sync, squeezing the air bag and then doing chest compressions on count like they were creating a rhythm. The paramedic who was doing the chest compressions stopped, reached in her bag, and pulled out a device that she used to cut a small hole in my son's leg. Again, I asked, "Why isn't my son breathing?" but my question went unanswered. The other paramedic never stopped squeezing the air mask during this time. They were moving fast and steadily, and I knew things were critical. But surely God wasn't about to let this happen. Although the gym was full of people, I could only see my son and the paramedics. It was like I had tunnel vision. I stood there helplessly as the paramedic strategically placed the stickers on my son's chest and said, "Clear!" as they shocked my son. The other paramedic continued to squeeze the air bag. The next thing I knew, the paramedics rolled my son onto a stretcher, looked at each other, and said, "We have to go now!" They were moving so fast, and I was right on their heels. Wherever they were going, so was I. As they rushed out the gym heading toward the ambulance that was right outside the door, I told them I was riding with them. One of the paramedics tried to tell me I couldn't, but rather than having an argument with me when I told her I wasn't leaving my son, she conceded. As the doors of the recreation center swung open, I saw my other sister pulling up. She ran up to me crying and screaming as they loaded my son onto the ambulance. I told her I had to go, that Tyrell still wasn't breathing, and I asked her to please go back to the house to get my daughter. Just as I sat down in the ambulance, I saw my mom standing there with my sisters, and I could see the fear and concern on all their faces as well.

As we rode in the ambulance, speeding through every light, I called my son's father to let him know what was happening, but he didn't answer his cell phone. He worked nights, so I knew it wasn't unusual for him not to answer. I called his wife, and she answered with her normal reluctant demeanor; I told her that I needed to speak to my son's father and that it was urgent. I told her that I was in the ambulance with Tyrell and he wasn't breathing. I asked her to get in touch with his dad and have him call me. Before I could hang the phone up, my son's father was calling me. I told him that Tyrell had collapsed while playing basketball and wasn't breathing. He asked me to repeat myself; I guess he was hoping that he had heard incorrectly. So, I said it again. "Tyrell isn't breathing!" He tried to be encouraging by telling me everything was going to be OK. I wanted to believe him; I needed to believe him. But as I turned around and saw that the paramedic was continuously doing CPR, I knew that couldn't be good. I kept telling Tyrell's father that they were still doing chest compressions.

He said, "That's good; they're still working on him."

I frantically said, "No! If he was breathing on his own, they would stop!" It took everything in my power to remain in my seat. I felt like I should've been doing something. I felt helpless and scared beyond belief. Tears were falling from my eyes as fast as I wiped them away. There was no way this was happening. This was my only son, the first person to make me a mother. He was my first child, and surely God wasn't about to take him from me. I was a nervous wreck and wanted so desperately to be at the hospital already. Someone had to help my baby!

The ambulance finally pulled into the hospital. Honestly, I don't even remember getting out of the ambulance. I just remember being inside the hospital and watching as the paramedics rushed my son down the hall and into room A2. It's crazy what stands out in your mind when things are happening. I didn't know it then, but that room number would forever be etched in my mind. As much as I wanted to go in the room with him, I was told that they needed to work on my son, and I was taken to a small, would-be waiting room that looked more like a small conference room. A nurse asked me to have a seat and told me that someone would be with me. I was alone and scared, and there was no way I could sit down. I wanted to know that my son was OK; I needed to be with him. So many thoughts were running through my head. I kept praying and pleading with God to make everything OK. This was by far the worst experience in my life. I didn't know what to think, how to act, or what to do. I was terrified! Ironically, every emotion I was feeling was internal. On the outside, I looked worried but in control, even though I wanted to scream and cry out. I kept thinking that God wouldn't take my baby. There's no way he would do that to me. That would be way more than I could handle, and over the course of my life I had been through a lot. I was always told that God wouldn't put more on you than you could bear, but losing my son would be unbearable. Just as I was trying to convince myself that everything would be OK, that maybe my son would have to be admitted to the hospital for a few days but surely he would be OK, I saw the doctor and a nurse walking toward me as I paced back and forth. I had seen enough movies to know that it couldn't be a good sign if the doctor and nurse were coming toward me. They both had serious looks on their faces, almost like they were afraid to approach me. I tried not to make eye contact as they walked toward me, in hopes that they would walk right past me.

My heart was beating so fast and hard that I could feel every heartbeat throughout my entire body. As they approached with the look of concern on their faces, I knew I was in for the shock of a lifetime. Then those words flowed off the doctor's lips as if he had rehearsed them. "I'm sorry. We did all we could." He continued to speak, but I couldn't hear anything else he was saying to me. I felt like life had been sucked out of my body, and I wanted more than anything to wake up from the horrible nightmare. Surely, I had to be in a terrible dream. There's no way my son, my only son, was dead! I had just seen him. He had just kissed me and told me he loved me.

My entire body was shaking, and I felt as if I were going to be sick. I didn't want to hear anything else the doctor was trying to say to me. He had said enough. I looked at the doctor, and I could see his lips moving, but there was still no sound. Everything around me turned white. At some point my sister was allowed to come back there. I don't remember seeing her walk up; I just knew that she was there telling me to get up off the floor. I did not pass out; I just dropped to my knees when the doctor said my son was gone. I pleaded for them to take me to my son. I didn't want to hear anything else they had to say. I just needed to see my baby.

Two

There it was! The most unimaginable moment: the thing that could only be described as a parent's worst nightmare. Only this was as real as it would get for me. My son! My only son, my first child, a senior in high school and destined for college, lay lifeless on a hospital bed! I walked slowly toward him, hoping that by the time I made it to his bedside he would start breathing. But I couldn't be that lucky. They had the white sheet pulled up to his chest, and he looked as if he was in a deep sleep. I could not stop kissing his face and laying my face on his chest. I was in such disbelief and extreme pain that I couldn't even cry, think, or speak. My desires were simple; I wanted him to start breathing, and I wanted to hold my son in my arms.

Before I knew it, there were many people in the room with my son and me and in the close-by waiting room that the hospital had designated for our family and friends. From the moment the doctor and nurse told me my son had passed, I don't remember a moment ever being alone with him. I really wanted and needed for everyone to leave the room, if only for a few minutes, to allow me to process things. But I couldn't tell them that; the lifelong habit of me thinking about everyone else superseded my need to have that alone time. I knew that everyone was hurting, and I didn't want to disregard their feelings of wanting to pay homage to my son and the family. People were crying and screaming; my daughters were inconsolable at times and quiet other times. I did what I was accustomed to: I held my pain inside and focused on making sure everyone else was OK. I didn't allow one tear to fall, a very bad habit I had developed as a child—the inability to cry or express pain or disappointment around others. As always during emotional or tense moments, I was quiet and just tried to push my feelings to the side, so much so that my body started to show the emotions that I couldn't. I remember hearing my daughter screaming and crying while everyone was trying to hug and console her, to no avail. After a few minutes of listening to her cries, I walked toward her, fighting my way through the crowd. Once I reached her, I didn't know what else to do, so I just closed my eyes and put my arms around her, hoping that the little strength I had left would be relinquished to her. I remember feeling dizzy, as if I was on a rapidly spinning Ferris Wheel that I desperately wanted to get off, but I failed at every attempt. It didn't take long for me to go from feeling dizzy to feeling light as a feather floating on a cloud. Without warning and with my daughter in my arms, I started to fall backward. I could no longer feel my legs, and I felt like the air was literally leaving my body. When I came to, I was on the floor, and a nurse was checking my blood pressure.

It was at that moment that the doctor said I would need to be admitted, because my blood pressure was so high and because I had lost consciousness. Mind you, I had never had high blood pressure, but I guess our bodies reveal the stressors we try so desperately to hide. I had never gone through anything like this in my life. The closest family member I'd ever lost was my brother-in-law many years before—but never the loss of someone I was used to seeing and talking to every day or on a regular basis. So, when the doctors recommended my being admitted in the hospital, I refused. I had just lost my only son; the last thing I was going to do was lie in a hospital, closed in with only my thoughts, pain, and the extreme urge to be sedated so I wouldn't have to think about anything at all. The doctor tried the next best thing and instructed my family to take me home for my own well-being.

I was so lost. I didn't know what I was supposed to be doing. I asked how long my son would be in the room, and I was told that he would remain there until I told them to take him to the morgue. In shock, my heart started racing even faster, and instant fear flowed through my veins. I looked my sister in her eyes, and she knew exactly what I was thinking. How could I tell someone to take my son and put him a cold freezer? Tears began to fill my eyes as I looked upon his face. I looked at the tattoo on his arm, which he had been so happy to get, and I kept thinking that this couldn't be real. My baby was lying there lifeless. No breaths; no more laughter. The only thing that would remain were my tears, at least the few that I was able to shed. Staring into my eyes, my sister gave me the look of assurance that indicated she would take care of it. Looking back on it now, I probably put way too much on her. But there was no way I could make that decision. There was no way I could form my mouth to say, "You can take him now." I knew it, and my sister knew it as well, and we were able to communicate that to one another without saying a word.

Before leaving the hospital, the doctor and a nurse pulled me to the side to make sure I wanted to have an autopsy performed on my son. The doctor said that it was clear that my son was athletic based on his body structure and muscle tone. He went on to say that although my son suffered from controlled asthma, he thought it would be best to be sure of the cause of death. The doctor said there could have been underlying conditions that could have caused my son's sudden death; some of those conditions were related to sudden death in teenage athletes who were seemingly healthy; so, an autopsy would be best. I agreed to have the autopsy done. I signed off on the paperwork for the autopsy and left the hospital shortly thereafter.

With my family by my side, I made it through the planning of the funeral and the funeral itself. Most of it was a blurred window of pain, anguish, disappointment, disbelief, anger, and many thoughts of sleeping to never awaken again. Although I wanted to cry and needed to cry, I could only allow a few tears to fall here and there. Part of me felt that if I were able give in to the tears and pain, I wouldn't be able to stop and would be forcibly admitted to a psychiatric facility.

My family helped me plan the funeral down to every detail—from the mime performance that my nephews did, to the songs performed by the youth choir my son had sung with every summer when he visited Huntsville before we moved here. Every detail about the funeral service represented who he was as a person. I walked around like a complete zombie the morning of the funeral. I was still in shock. We gathered at my sister's house in preparation for the funeral procession. I remember walking into the cathedral, and there was standing room only. People were standing outside the megachurch and in the foyer because there were no seats available. I remember sitting on the church pew feeling like I was in a bad dream. I couldn't believe I was staring at my son's lifeless body in that casket. I could hear screams that seemed so distant even though they were all around me, some of them coming from my daughters and sisters who sat next to me. Although there was standing room only, and people were next to and behind me, my focus was on the bedlike casket and pillow that encompassed my son. All I wanted to do was look at my son's face for as long as I could.

I remember the funeral director coming and telling me they needed to close the casket because it was causing unrest among the attendees. I couldn't believe she said that to me. Did she really think I was concerned about anyone else in that moment? I did not want the casket closed; I'd made that clear when we were planning the funeral. As the service moved on and the floor was opened to allow people to say a few words about my son and how they remembered him, I wasn't sure of what to expect to hear, considering some of the people who asked to speak were friends who only knew my son for a few years. A couple of stories grabbed my attention more than others as my mind faded the sounds in and out. There was one in particular by an elderly man, who spoke about his encounter with my son and how he and his wife would go to the movie theater where my son worked every Friday, just to see him. He spoke of how my son always smiled and would help his wife to her seat, calling her beautiful the entire time. The other story was that of a teenager who said he first met my son at a track meet. This young man had left his cleats and was going to have to forfeit his race if he didn't find some shoes to wear. He said he asked several people, including students from his high school, to allow him to use their shoes for the race, but no one would. He said he never asked my son, but although they attended different schools and were considered rivals, my son had overheard him asking others and walked up to him and told him he could use his shoes. In the words of the young man, my son "literally gave me the shoes off his feet." I couldn't help but smile, because I knew my son was a loving and giving person. In spite of my agony, it was nice to hear others, strangers in fact, talk about their experience of the compassion my son had for others. As I smiled inside from the way everyone spoke of my son, I also felt more sadness, because I knew that my earthy angel was gone.

The church was still in an uproar, and the screams and outbursts quickly brought me back to the present moment. Those stories hit home for so many people who knew my son. Everyone was crying and screaming, and I could only sit there staring at my son's face. So many thoughts were running through my head. I was shaking like a leaf, and I didn't know how I was supposed to be conducting myself. Once again, the lady from the funeral home came to me to say that we really needed to close the casket. My blood immediately started boiling! I looked in her in her eyes while clenching my teeth and told her not to ask me to close the casket again. Selfish or not, I didn't care how anyone else felt; I just wanted to look at my son's face for as long as I could. She was concerned about how others were feeling, but I think if she had closed that casket, I would have lost my mind completely.

It astounds me what your mind decides to hold on to and what it chooses to release, because I don't remember leaving the church nor driving to the burial ground. I just remember sitting there and looking at my son's casket being lowered into the ground. As they lowered his casket, I felt like the air was being sucked out my body, and for the life of me I couldn't stop shaking. My entire body was trembling, maybe because his death was becoming final, maybe because I didn't want to let him go. I didn't know how I would ever be able to let him go. For me, goodbye was forever, and I refused to allow those words to flow from my mouth. I didn't know how to release the pain that felt like it was going to consume me more and more as each second passed. Although I had been hurt many times in my life, nothing prepared me for the death of my son. I was completely lost. I didn't know how to act or what to think, and unfortunately, I didn't know how to feel.

Many people came up to hug me and offer their condolences. I smiled and thanked each of them, because that seemed like the right thing to do. I held on to my daughters for dear life, hoping I could be strong for them. Everyone was standing around the burial site, taking pictures and swapping stories. It was very overwhelming to me, and I asked the funeral director if we could go back to the church for the repast. My shaking had turned into nausea and dizziness. I figured it was from emotions and the fact that I hadn't eaten breakfast; honestly, I hadn't consumed much food at all since the night this tragedy struck my life. But by the time we got back to the church, it had gotten worse. Next thing I knew, I was stretched out on a bench with people standing all around me. Once again, I had collapsed. This time it was because my blood sugar had dropped too low, a common reaction when someone who is hypoglycemic doesn't consume enough nutrients. Unlike most people, when I am hurting or sad, my appetite is the first thing to go, which is attributed to my being hypoglycemic. When I came to, the ambulance was there, and my sugar was so low that they insisted on taking me to the hospital; naturally, I refused.

Three

The next few weeks after the funeral were a blur. I found myself going through the motions of day-to-day activities. I spent most of my time at my friend's house, because I felt like it was my only escape and the only place that didn't have constant reminders of my son everywhere. I kept playing back the night of my son's death and wondered what really took place. Many people contacted me after he died, saying that they kept asking the people at the recreation center to help my son after he collapsed, but no one did. I couldn't believe that to be true, but I knew I was going to do all I could to find out.

A couple of weeks after my son's death, I decided to drive up to the place where it all happened, the Richard Showers Center. I walked through the doors and, like the tragic night of my son's death, no one greeted me or asked me if they could be of assistance. I walked to the gym, nervous and uncertain, but I was curious to see if there were any CPR or first aid posters anywhere that could have guided someone to help my son. I also looked around for a defibrillator, which is a lifesaving device used to shock the heart of a person whose heart suddenly stops. Surely, a recreation center would have one on site.

I made my way to the front office and informed two gentleman who I was and why I was there. They introduced themselves as supervisors and stated that they were there the night of my son's death, but they couldn't speak with me. I was shocked and continued to say that I was there because of the reports of no one offering to help my dying son. I told them that I did see the defibrillator in their front office and that I couldn't understand why they didn't use it. They repeated that they were instructed not to talk to me because of the possibility of a lawsuit.

Lawsuit? I thought. Who was thinking about a lawsuit, when my son had only been dead for about three weeks? I wanted clarification and to dispel the rumors that they did absolutely nothing to try and help my son. But they wouldn't speak. Fine. But I was going to get answers one way or another. I called Dr. Richard Showers's office to see if he could give me some answers on why his staff at his facility had failed to help my son. I called and left countless messages, none of which were ever returned. But I wasn't going to stop, no matter what. A few days later, I received a call from a reporter asking me questions about my son's death. He said that he too had gone to the Richard Showers Center to question the staff on the events surrounding my son's death, but they had refused to speak with him as well.

He said he had contacted Dr. Showers but was told that "he didn't know a Tyrell Spencer." Those words stung me like a bee. He didn't know "a" Tyrell Spencer—as if my son was an object, not a person! The reporter clarified that the Richard Showers Center was owned by the City of Huntsville and was named after Dr. Showers. But it seemed to me that Dr. Showers could have had a better reaction to the fact that a child had died at a facility that carried his name—aside from the fact that he was a city councilman. As the days went by, I continued doing my research to prove the rumors true or false. I contacted the 911 dispatch office and paid for transcripts of the calls on the night of my son's death. I read the transcribed words of my fourteen-year-old daughter, who called 911 pleading for someone to get to the Richard Showers Center to help her brother who wasn't breathing. I read the transcribed calls of an unknown caller asking for an ambulance at the Richard Showers Center as well. The problem with this was that my daughter was the first person to call, and she was not even at the facility, while the second call came seven minutes after my daughter's call. *How was that possible?* I kept thinking.

I called the same reporter who initially told me about Dr. Showers and told him about my discovery. I was asked to do a live interview, which I agreed to do. I wanted people to know that the staff at that facility hadn't even tried to help my son or call 911. I didn't want this to happen to another parent, especially when a recreation center is staffed and supposed to be a safe haven for youth. I chose to do the interview in front of the Richard Showers Center. I made it clear that Dr. Showers would know who Tyrell Spencer was when I was done. The day my son was born, I looked him in his eyes for the first time and, like most mothers, I promised to love and protect him. Throughout his life I taught him the meaning of love and assured him that I would fight for him until the day I died, and this was no exception. I never imagined that my fight would be because of his death.

Throughout this horrible experience, I constantly wondered if my son had been afraid when he collapsed. I remembered that when he would have an asthma attack, even a mild one, he would panic, and I would have to calm him down and remind him to breathe. But from all accounts, no one had comforted him that night. Not one person. If God himself explained to me that he had to take my son but would grant me one thing, my plea would've been for me to have been by my son's side to hold him, comfort him, and make sure he knew he wasn't alone. He should've known that his mother was right there with him. Maybe that would have given me some form of comfort as well. The pain of not being by his side will torture me for the rest of my life. I not only have the agony of losing my one and only son, but I am angry knowing that not one staff member at this facility made any attempts to help my baby. Even a dog will lick and put its paw on you if you fall in front of it; so, what does that say for the staff and onlookers? More so, what does that say for how they viewed my lifeless son.?

All my pain was superseded by anger and determination. I was determined to make Dr. Showers and the city that owned the Richard Showers Center acknowledge their wrong. Not because I wanted money—it wasn't about that at all. There is no amount of money that could make me feel better about my son's death or assist me in dealing with his death. It was about acknowledging Tyrell Spencer, since Dr. Showers made a point to say he didn't know "a" Tyrell Spencer. Secondly, and most importantly, I wanted them to publicly admit that their staff did not handle the situation properly and to ensure that this wouldn't happen to another child.

My family and I held protests outside the Richard Showers Center, hoping to show that we were not going to let them get away with not helping my son. After two years of protesting, calls, and interviews, the acknowledgement I had been seeking came on January 11, 2013, when the City of Huntsville, the mayor, and Dr. Showers presented me with a memorial plaque and also unveiled a memorial plaque outside the gym where my son laid helpless on the night of November 17, 2010.

Although I finally had the public acknowledgment of my son that I had been seeking, I didn't have the heart to speak, because I would have spoken from anger, and that was not the time or place. So, I asked my sister to speak at the dedication in my place. My mom always taught me that if I didn't have anything nice to say, then I shouldn't say anything at all. So, for that moment I used silence as my weapon. I was greeted by the mayor, and he asked to take a picture with me, which I kindly agreed to. I just couldn't find it in myself to fake a smile. The news media and my family were present. This should have been the end of my fighting, but during my fight with the city, I discovered that an autopsy had never been conducted on my son. Although I did a little probing as to why the autopsy hadn't been done, my focus at the time was on addressing the recreation center and bringing awareness of their lack of response to an on-site emergency situation, a response that could have possibly prevented the death of my son.

Once the dedication was complete, I started actively pursuing options to determine the actual cause of death for my son and to figure out why the autopsy had never been conducted. From the day my son died, my life flipped upside down. As if his death weren't tragic enough, I had to deal with fighting the City of Huntsville as well as the endless quest to answer the question of what really caused his untimely death.

Death does strange things to people, and people react differently to their pain. Some accept it and move on, some become severely depressed, and some people act out, while others may turn to the church, drugs, and alcohol. Whatever method is chosen, to me, they are all coping mechanisms, because there is no way to honestly deal with the pain of death—especially that of your child. The death of my son was the straw that broke the camel's back for me. My faith changed, my life changed, and my relationship with my family changed. I withdrew from everyone. I resisted anything that would remind me that my son was gone and being around family did just that. I didn't know how to be around my family and not have my son there. The few times I did try, I would expect my son to walk in the room and dance or crack a joke, and when he didn't, I wanted to scream. And because I couldn't allow myself to scream, I would have major anxiety attacks.

My family didn't understand my absence, and I didn't have the strength to explain it to them. While I did not want to go to the familiar places with my family, I still desired to see them or hear from them from time to time. Not long after my son's death, my boyfriend and I moved in together. It was easier for me to do things at my house than it was for me to go to my family's houses, places I had been hundreds of times with my son. Unfortunately, my family took my not coming around and my telling them that I couldn't handle being around them as me not desiring to be around them, and that made them feel like that was the best thing for me. In actuality, I needed them and wished they would put forth an effort and ignore what I said and force themselves on me. It hurt me that they would rarely call or check up on me, and that put a barrier between us all on top of the pain of losing my son. Also, my family wasn't completely aware of the probing I was doing to figure out why the autopsy hadn't been done. Maybe if they had known, it would have helped them to understand that the loss of my son, the public acknowledgement from the city, and the pain of my son's absence weren't the only things I was dealing with. That bit of information would've changed their perception of who I had become, although I was still learning who I was supposed to be.

My son's death was and is the most extreme thing I think I will ever experience. But his death isn't the only tragedy to this story. My son was a healthy high school senior who suffered from occasional asthma attacks; he rarely required the use of his inhaler and was a star athlete. The night of his death, as I mentioned earlier in this story, the doctors told me that I really should have an autopsy performed. They said there were illnesses that cause sudden death in athletes as well as underlying heart conditions that I may need to know about in order protect my daughters from suffering a similar fate. According to the ER doctor, none of these possible concerns are found in routine health exams. If you remember, I ordered the autopsy and signed the paperwork before leaving the hospital the night of my son's death. However, I didn't find out that the autopsy hadn't been conducted until my son was buried and I received the death certificate with "undetermined" as the cause of death.

How could I grieve when I didn't know why my baby had died suddenly and without warning? How could I move on when I had the fear that this could possibly happen to one of my other two children? This began my next round of fighting. After researching, it was discovered that the hospital's pathology lab had made a mistake and taken my son off the autopsy schedule and never put him back on. Yes, you read this correctly. I ordered the autopsy, my son was put on the schedule to have the autopsy conducted, and he was removed, to be put in a different time slot, but was never put back on the schedule. This wasn't discovered until I started probing, calling the hospital, and pulling hospital records. Of course, my probing was because I couldn't understand why the death certificate said, "undetermined cause of death." My first thought was that the autopsy results weren't available at the time the death certificate was generated. Again, keep in mind that I had never dealt with anything like this in my entire life. I didn't know what was normal and what was not. I felt like there was no way I would go through the rest of my life with the lingering question of how and why my son died. No parent should have to go through that.

This added to what was already an unbearable amount of pain, and honestly, I didn't want to live. I didn't necessarily want to die either; I just wanted the pain to stop—even if that meant I no longer existed. The only thing that kept me from taking my own life was the love I have for my daughters. There was no way I could do that to them. They needed me. Whatever part of me that was left, my daughters deserved to have me.

I knew they would never have me completely until I figured out my options with the hospital, and time was of the essence. I spoke to several attorneys in Huntsville, and each one of them explained that I had a good case against the hospital, but it would take a lot of money to go up against a hospital of that size. I refused to give up, even if I had to fight this one alone as well. I finally found an attorney in Birmingham, Alabama, who offered to take my case. He filed the formal lawsuit but later dropped the case for the same reasons as the other attorneys. So, I continued the fight on my own. I was called in for depositions by the hospital's attorneys, and they tried to put a great deal of pressure on me to drop the case.

I was out of my element, but I wasn't going to let them talk me down. My primary concern and request were for them to cover the cost of exhuming my son's body and performing the autopsy that they should have done, but everything I asked landed on deaf ears. Initially, I didn't know that exhumation was an option until I was watching television late one night where a person's body was exhumed to do a DNA test. That was the moment I remembered all the CSI episodes and crime shows that I had watched over the years and how they could find a person's body in the woods and still determine a cause of death. So, I started looking into exhumation and forensic pathology. I called every pathology lab, medical school, and anyone who could give me insight on the process. One thing I found out very quickly was that it was very expensive. It would cost more to exhume my son's body and have the autopsy performed than it did to bury him. I felt like it was me against the world; I was weak, hurting, and in need of some form of antivenom, if there were such a thing.

About one week before the court date, I made an offer to settle the case, and the hospital accepted it. Unfortunately, the settlement amount was insulting and a very small fraction of the cost of the exhumation, autopsy, and reburial. But I was fearful of going to court and walking away with nothing at all. As part of the settlement, I had to agree to never disclose the settlement amount, and if asked about the case, I could only legally say that we reached an agreement. As I think back on it now, I wish I would have gone to court, if for no other reason than to allow the judge to hear what happened and to make his or her decision. But I allowed my fear to make me feel that it was better to have something over nothing at all, with the hopes of using the agreed amount to exhume my son on my own.

Four

Once the case was settled, I continued to call pathology labs and medical schools, hoping that someone would have sympathy enough to donate their time to perform the autopsy. Unfortunately, I have yet to find that one person or group of people. I emailed every organization and medical television show; believe it or not, I even emailed Oprah, Ellen DeGeneres, Steve Harvey—you name it, I tried it. When you are desperate, you are willing to try anything. I have constant nightmares about digging up my son's grave in the middle of the night using only my hands, feeling like it would bring enough media attention that someone would step in and grant me closure. Honestly, a large part of me feels like I failed him somehow. I know that I fought the best way I knew how, and I still lost in the end, but I am always left wondering if there is something more I could have done.

I raised him well. He was kind, loving, funny, and undeserving of the way his life ended. My heart aches on a constant basis.

Although years have passed since his death, I still hurt as if it happened yesterday. I still struggle with being around my family, but I have vowed to do better. The one thing I can feel proud about since the death of my son is that I can honestly say he knew I loved him. I don't have to be tortured with thoughts of *I wish I would've* or *I wish I could've*. I showed him genuine love every day of his life, and that is my motivation with my family. I don't want to ever be in a situation where something happens and all I'm left with is *I wish I would have*.

These earth-shattering events changed my relationship with God. I grew up in the church, and I know enough to know that I don't hate God. I like to say he and I just have a misunderstanding that we are working through. It showed in the way I prayed for my son's life to be spared, the way I prayed for a door or window to be opened so my son could be exhumed to have that autopsy done, and the way I prayed for peace and comfort. I don't know how God can do that to me. I don't question him; I simply don't understand, and that makes it hard for me to attend church or listen to gospel music, which used to be one of my favorite forms of music. I don't go to church often, and I haven't listed to gospel music in years, because it evokes another level of pain that I prefer not to deal with. I will not allow anyone or any situation to cause me to denounce God.

I'm learning to take one step at a time and not try to force anything on myself. When you have lost a child, you also have to learn that it is OK not to be OK. We cause more harm to ourselves by trying to be what people think we should or what they want us to be. We are allowed to be selfish; we are allowed to feel however we need to feel to get through this moment so we can deal with the next moment. This is what I work on each day while I continue to turn the hundred no's of having my son's autopsy done to one yes. My tears still don't fall, and I don't think they will until I have closure. That closure will not come until I can one day exhume my son's body and get the answers to his sudden death. My struggle is a constant one. I know my true peace will not come until I know the cause of my son's death, and I'm starting to face the harsh reality that *I may never know.*

Parent to Parent

There are no clear ways to deal with the loss of someone you love, and it's an even harder battle when that someone is your child. The loss of my son was beyond hard on me and was by far the worst tragedy in my life. I personally struggle with letting go and allowing myself to grieve. Our bodies are designed to release pain, and when we hold it inside, it is going to force its way out one way or another. Mine happens to show its ugly face through the inability to sleep, nightmares, and anxiety attacks. I speak from experience, because I have trained myself to hold in my pain since I was a teenager. Your mind will force you to address your problems, even in your subconscious. A large part of me thought that acting like I was OK was me being strong for my daughters; now I realize how I was hurting them. I didn't show them that it is OK to hurt and to release their pain, because I didn't know and still don't know how to release my own.

I still don't speak of my son in the past tense. It's like my mind won't let go of him. It is still very hard for me to drive past his grave, and the only time I can visit his gravesite is when I can disassociate from reality. It's like an out-of-body experience where I am watch myself wipe off the grave and put new flowers down. It's a mental separation and one of many coping mechanisms. I hurt every moment of every day, and no matter how busy I am, my son is in the back of my mind, like a movie that won't stop playing regardless of the activities taking place around me.

Although I don't understand why God chose to take my son, I work diligently to try to find solace in his decision. I constantly look for some logic to this madness. Unfortunately, grief has a mind of its own. But I have found it helpful to review personal quotes that I have written over the years, based on how I felt at random times. It is my hope that my words can resonate with others, so they don't feel as lost and alone as I have all these years. You have to accept the bad moments as much as you accept the good and know that it's OK. Iyanla Vanzant wrote, "When a woman buries her child, everything she does is colored by that experience. When a woman buries a child, there's a hole in her soul that changes who she is."

Those words are very true. I am no longer the person I was before burying my child, and I will never become that person again. My pain is constant, and I believe I will hurt twenty years from now just as bad as I did the day he died. We have to find a way to release our pain, because through that release comes a little bit of relief. Talking to someone doesn't necessarily mean you have to go to a psychologist or counselor. You may be better off joining a group, talking to other parents who have lost a child, or finding someone you feel comfortable enough with to show the real side of you.

The point is to find a way to deal with the tragedies that we face so that we will not be haunted by them. Many people experience similar tragedies, but most keep their feelings to themselves without realizing that their story could save the life of another grieving parent. I encourage everyone to find their release and to reach out to me and others like me whenever they feel closed in, because those days will come, sometimes more frequently than others. Silence has a sound, and it can become very loud when you are alone or feel like you are alone. The pain you feel will drown out even the smallest piece of love and hope you thought you had, if you let it.

I hope expressing my pain and sharing my story helps you realize that we stand in solidarity. We share a bond that only we understand, for there is no greater pain than losing a child!

> Your thoughts have feelings! Write them down when speaking seems impossible.

- Don't give up; your pain could be the sunshine that saves the life of someone who relates to it.

- Some say I'm strong, others want the recipe to the glue that holds me together. Honestly, I'm not strong, and there is no recipe or glue for that matter. I hide behind the truth, telling myself that my son is on a long trip, until that lie fades and I succumb to anxiety, when the mental images of his lifeless body take over my mind and I realize he's *gone*!

- It's the smallest things that change my happy memories of my son from a smile to an overwhelming desire to scream. I ache because I know that I will never be able to form new memories, and when I think of the wonderful memories we had, it makes me long for more. There's no winning here.

- Sometimes I wish I could cry so hard. I've conditioned myself to avoid crying. It's such a bad habit. Sometimes healing comes through tears. It's OK to cry and it's OK to hurt, for you are human.

  _____

- I'd give anything to have my son here, living and breathing.

  _____

- We go through some horrible things in our lives but having a great support system makes all the difference in the world. Remember to be that support system even if you don't agree or understand. It's not always about you, and your compassion could save someone who feels like they are drowning.

  _____

- I wish family understood that my pulling away meant they should've tried harder to be present. Losing my son came with such deep pain that all I could do was hide within myself. We should not be judged by our "right now," but by what others know us to be. *Notice the difference?*

- I forget people's names, I forget the pot on the stove, and I forget the water running in the sink, yet I remember the day, the hour, and the minute my son was born and, tragically, when he died. There are some things a parent's mind holds on to.

- Sometimes you must look beyond the obvious. You never know what hides behind those with the biggest smiles and the largest personalities. I smile to comfort others and to make the crowded room of people feel comfortable. I'm the life of the party, or so I've been told, but if you really watch me, you will notice that my mind tends to drift, and I'm no longer mentally in the same room with anyone. It's those frequent moments when my mind is on my son.

- My son was the male who would always be in my life. His daily reminder was mere words to others but had unmeasurable value between him and me. "*I got you!*" I miss the endearing promise behind those words.